and just like that...

SOULFUL HOLIDAY RECIPES MADE EASY

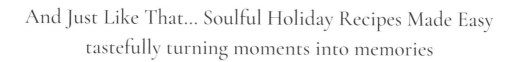

And Just Like That... Soulful Holiday Recipes Made Easy
tastefully turning moments into memories

written & photographed by @chefmikehard

ISBN: 979-8-9872465-2-8

10 9 8 7 6 5 4 3 2 1

First Edition

This cookbook is dedicated to my bloodline — past, present & future. I am because you were, are & will be. Bonds are broken, legacy is established & I remain grateful for the blessing yet humbled by the burden.

@chefmikehard

table of
CONTENTS

@chefmikehard

Introduction

Foreword

the recipes

Grandma Hattie's Oven Roasted Turkey   1

Uncle Marshall's Honey Baked Ham   5

Uncle Steve's Smothered Beef Roast   9

Nanny's Cornbread Dressing   13

Chef's Homemade Cranberry Sauce   17

Chef's Homestyle Pan Gravy   21

Auntie G's Deviled Eggs   25

Cousin Coco's Potato Salad   29

Mommy's Baked Mac 'n Cheese   33

Cousin Kim's Candied Yams   37

Chef's Garlic Parmesan Mashed Potatoes   41

Chef's Garlic Butter Green Beans   45

TT Dawn's Collard Greens   49

Chef's Buttermilk Cornbread   53

sweet treats

BONUS RECIPES

Nanny's Sweet Potato Pie 59

7 UP® Pound Cake 63

Whipped Banana Pudding 67

Brown Butter Peach Cobbler 71

Strawberry Crunch Cheesecake 75

Better Than Scratch Box Brownies 79

DoubleTree® Chocolate Chip Cookies 83

Introduction

What's the vibes?! Listen, I know you're ready to get started with cooking up these amazing, classic soul food recipes! I wanted to take a moment to say THANK YOU for supporting me on my very FIRST cookbook project.

This body of work is the culmination of a lifetime so far of flavors, influences & inspiration. You have no idea how much it means to me to have you be a part of my story!

So do me a quick favor and let me know you got your copy and are ready to vibe in the kitchen with me. Share a post or story on Instagram and definitely let me see those food photos once you start cooking. Don't forget to tag me @chefmikehard!

I've made the recipes as organized and clear as possible, and have even included vegan variations! So follow along and don't miss a beat. It always helps to read the whole recipe one time before you even get started cooking, so there are no surprises, no missed steps, and no forgotten ingredients.

There's also a link to my Amazon List for many of the kitchen tools and supplies you'll need to master every recipe. Just click the link in my Instagram bio to browse and shop my list on Amazon straight from your phone or computer, with fast delivery right to your doorstep!

Thanks again for choosing to let my holiday cookbook guide your #foodlove and welcome to the #VibeTribe!

@chefmikehard

Foreword

Chefs are often asked, "how did you start cooking?" I have been blessed to grow up around some amazing family cooks, so good food is something that has always been present for me.

I grew up watching my maternal grandmother serve as the Lead Cook at my childhood church. Watching her in the kitchen cooking in high volume while maintaining made-from-scratch flavor and most importantly the grace of hospitality.

I witnessed my paternal grandmother prepare holiday dinners for family, pulling on the experience of growing up with 17 siblings, then raising 9 children of her own on the south side of Chicago in a time where Black women were not fully allowed to just be, let alone be granted with fair opportunities to uplift.

I experienced my own working mother cook dinner for our family, while also meeting the demands of a 34 year long career in social work and always finding a way to make ends meet.

These experiences helped shape within me a strong appreciation for the power of food and the togetherness it creates. The ability for friends to become family; for family to gather, to celebrate, and to enjoy with love. That is my hope with this, my very first cookbook, for that same intention to be felt and experienced by all who are touched by my recipes.

Each of the 21 recipes found in this cookbook are @chefmikehard originals, inspired and influenced by #foodlove. The names of each recipe tell the story of who and how each of them came to be one of my personal favorites.

So I hope you enjoy these dishes as much as I do and that you experience #foodlove in your own way, as these recipes become *your* favorites while you share and cook with me. Let's Vibe!

@chefmikehard

GRANDMA HATTIE'S OVEN ROASTED TURKEY

My paternal grandmother's name was Hattie. That really should be all you need to know to determine whether or not she got busy in the kitchen! Growing up and visiting her house on holidays, there isn't a time I can remember where she didn't have that ceramic coated, speckled roasting pan sitting on the stove top. You could always count on opening that lid — after washing your hands of course — and revealing the most beautifully cooked Oven Roasted Turkey that everyone would slice off of as they made their plates under her watchful, approving gaze. Grandma Hattie never got to taste my version of Oven Roasted Turkey — although she absolutely loved my Black-Eyed Peas — but I believe she would have approved and I think you will too. Enjoy!

Ingredients

Roasted Turkey Seasoning
- 2-3 tablespoons sea salt, to taste
- 1/2 tablespoon black pepper
- 2 tablespoons granulated onion
- 1 tablespoon granulated garlic
- 1/2 tablespoon dried savory
- 1/2 tablespoon dried italian seasoning
- 1/2 tablespoon dried basil
- 1 tablespoon poultry seasoning
- 2 teaspoons paprika
- 4 sticks butter

Brine
- 1/4 cup sea salt
- 1/4 cup white sugar
- 1 cup lemon juice
- 2.5 gallons water

- **12-14 lb Turkey, thawed**

Step-by-Step Instructions

5 Days Before Cooking...
- Thaw packaged frozen turkey in fridge for 3 days before using
- Take note (or a cell phone photo) of packaged turkey weight

2 Days Before Cooking...
- After thawing 3 days take turkey out of packaging, removing any ice or parts from inside cavity of turkey
- Mix brine ingredients in a large bucket or container that will fit in your fridge
- Add turkey to brine bucket/container & allow to soak in brine for 48 hours, inside fridge

Day of Cooking...
- After 48 hours, remove turkey from brine, discarding brine liquid
- Rinse turkey under cold water & pat dry with paper towels, including inside cavity
- Combine Roast Turkey Seasoning ingredients in a small pan & heat until butter is just melted
- Spread seasoning mixture all over turkey, as well as under skin & inside cavity
- Tuck turkey wings, then cross & tie turkey legs before putting seasoned turkey in roasting pan
- Remove highest rack(s) from oven & preheat to 450 degrees F
- Roast turkey uncovered for 20 min at 450 degrees F
- After 20 minutes do not open oven
- Reduce heat to 250 degrees F & do not open oven
- Continue to cook turkey at 250 degrees F for 18 min per 1 lb of packaged turkey weight
  - Example: 12 lb turkey will cook for 20 min at 450 degrees F then 216 min (3 hours, 36 min) at 250 degrees F
- After cook time is complete remove turkey from oven, cover with foil & let rest for 1 hour
- Check for doneness with using instant read stem thermometer in thickest parts of turkey breast (170 degrees F) & thigh (180 degrees F)
- Turkey will still be hot & juicy after resting time
- Turkey can be carved & served after resting or cooled & refrigerated to serve the next day

Pro Tips!

- Trust the process!

- Cook times & temps are not typos.

- Yes, turkey can be cooked from cold.

- No, turkey does not need to be brought to room temp before cooking.

- No, turkey does not need to be seasoned ahead of time but prepping ahead does save time.

- No, turkey does not need to be covered while cooking.

- Yes, turkey can be covered with a sheet of foil after 1 hour, to avoid over browning.

- No, turkey does not have to be basted while it cooks since it was brined.

- No, do not cook turkey in a bag.

- No, do not stuff the inside of the turkey.

- Yes, tuck the wings of the turkey so they don't over cook.

- Yes, cross & tie the legs of the turkey so they don't over cook.

- When checking temperature for doneness, make sure to insert thermometer into meat only & do not touch bone.

UNCLE MARSHALL'S HONEY BAKED HAM

Now this recipe may not be for everybody, but in our family, swine is just fine! The Thanksgiving table is not complete without a sweet & savory Honey Baked Ham courtesy of Uncle Marshall. Now Unc can make that ham and make it right, but you better believe he is most likely buying it from his favorite grocery store, then dropping it off for somebody else to make and bring! Ain't nothing wrong with that Unc, as long as we got it. Just make sure somebody takes that ham-bone home to make ham salad or a pot of beans with later in the week!

Ingredients

- 8-10 lb spiral cut ham
- 1 can cored pineapple slices
- 1 jar maraschino cherries, stems removed

Seasoning Blend
- 1 teaspoon sea salt
- 1/2 teaspoon black pepper
- 1/2 cup brown sugar
- 1/2 teaspoon ground cloves
- 1 tablespoon cornstarch

Wet Ingredients
- 1/2 cup honey
- 2 tablespoons bourbon whiskey
- pineapple juice from slices
- 1/4 cup juice from cherries
- 1/2 stick butter

Step-by-Step Instructions

- Measure & combine seasoning blend in a dish & set aside

- Measure & combine wet ingredients in a pan & place over medium/low heat

- Add already combined seasoning blend to heated wet ingredients & stir to combine

- Unpackage spiral cut ham then place in a baking dish

- Pour heated sauce mixture over ham, making sure to get sauce in all cracks & crevices

- Using toothpicks to secure, evenly place pineapple slices all over ham & top each toothpick with a maraschino cherry

- Cover ham in baking dish loosely with foil

- Preheat oven to 325 degrees F

- Cook ham for 15 minutes per pound at 325 degrees F

  - Example: An 8 lb ham will cook for 120 minutes (2 hours)

- Baste ham with juices from bottom of pan approximately every 30 minutes while cooking

- After cook time is complete, allow ham to rest covered for 30 minutes.

- Slice & enjoy with extra pan drippings & a scoop of potato salad!

Pro Tips!

- You can sub a bone-in ham for a boneless cut, just slice before cooking.

- After cooking, it helps with serving to slice ham off of bone.

- Don't forget to use those leftovers for ham & eggs, ham sandwiches, ham salad, or stewed with a pot of beans!

UNCLE STEVE'S SMOTHERED BEEF ROAST

Each one of my mother's three brothers can cook! After all, they learned from one of the best — their mom & my grandmother. Uncle Steve is best known in the family for his ribs; always and only baby backs are coming off of his grill. But make no mistake, Unc has range in the kitchen. Over the years, his Smothered Beef Roast has become a staple for holiday family gatherings. That tender, savory flavor is the definition of comfort food, so I had to share my recipe with you for your holiday table. And don't worry, my Garlic Parmesan Mashed Potatoes are coming up in a few pages because, of course!

Ingredients

- **3 lbs chuck roast, cut in chunks**

Sautée Ingredients
- 2 tablespoons butter
- 1 tablespoon cooking oil
- 2 carrots, sliced
- 2 ribs celery, diced
- 1 onion, chopped
- 1 green bell pepper, chopped
- 4 cloves garlic, chopped

Gravy Mix
- 1/2 cup cornstarch
- 3/4 cup cold water
- 1 tablespoon browning

Seasoning Blend
- 1 tablespoon sea salt
- 1/2 tablespoon black pepper
- 1 tablespoon granulated onion
- 1/2 tablespoon granulated garlic
- 1/2 teaspoon celery salt
- 1 teaspoon dried thyme leaves
- 1/2 tablespoon beef bouillon
- 3 bay leaves

Wet Ingredients
- 2 bottles stout beer
- 2 cups beef broth
- 1/4 cup white vinegar
- 1/4 cup soy sauce
- 2 tablespoons worcestershire

Step-by-Step Instructions

- Except bay leaves, measure & combine all seasoning blend ingredients in a small dish & set aside

- Combine wet ingredients in a mixing bowl or large enough dish & set aside

- Preheat oven to 350 degrees F, unless using an InstantPot

- In a mixing bowl drizzle about 2 tablespoons cooking oil (like avocado) over large cut chunks of chuck roast

- Add seasoning blend to chuck roast, using tongs to toss & evenly coat

- Sear seasoned chunks of chuck roast in 2 tablespoons cooking oil in a large dutch oven over medium/high heat or InstantPot until each piece is lightly brown on all sides & set aside in a separate dish

- In same dutch oven or InstantPot add butter & cooking oil from sautée ingredients & allow butter to melt

- Except garlic, add remaining sautée ingredients & cook 5 minutes while stirring

- After 5 minutes add garlic & continue cooking 2 minutes while stirring

- After 2 minutes add already combined wet ingredients to dutch oven or InstantPot, scraping bits from bottom of pan

- Add seared chuck roast chunks to & bay leaves, wet & sautée ingredients already in dutch oven or InstantPot

- Placed covered dutch oven in the oven at 350 degrees F for 2 hours or until beef roast is fork tender or cover InstantPot & cook on high pressure for 45 minutes

- Allow InstantPot to natural release for 15 minutes before pushing button to release remaining pressure

- Remove beef roast from pot to a serving dish, cover with foil & set aside

- Thicken juices with combined gravy mixture over medium/high heat while stirring until desired gravy thickness & add salt + pepper or seasonings to taste

- Smother beef roast with pan gravy in serving dish & enjoy!

Pro Tips!

- Always chop, slice & dice vegetable & produce ingredients before you start cooking.

- Always measure & combine seasonings before you start cooking.

- Do not crowd pan when searing chuck roast; sear in batches if needed.

- When sautéing always add garlic later so it doesn't burn & taste bitter.

- Natural release for InstantPot/pressure cooker means letting it just sit untouched after the cooktime.

- Manual release means pressing the pressure release button to let out remaining pressure before removing cover.

- If gravy is too thick, add water/broth to loosen.

- If gravy is too thin, allow to cook longer to reduce or add more cornstarch mixture to tighten up.

NANNY'S CORNBREAD DRESSING

In our family, Cornbread Dressing is king and my grandmother — Nanny as we called her — was the queen of making it! Without a doubt, this is my absolute favorite recipe in this cookbook. There wasn't a family gathering or church basement event without a pan of Nanny's famous Cornbread Dressing. It was smooth, creamy, aromatic, and savory. Pure soul food perfection. Dressing is one of the first recipes I made it a point to learn from Nanny and I am so glad I did. Nanny has since gone to rest in Heaven, but when it comes to Thanksgiving now, my family looks to me to bring the Dressing, which is the highest form of praise. If you like Dressing you will love my recipe...over and over again!

Ingredients

Sautée Ingredients
- 2 tablespoons butter
- 1 tablespoon cooking oil
- 1/2 onion, diced
- 2 ribs celery, diced
- 1 green bell pepper, diced
- 1/2 teaspoon dried thyme leaves
- 1/2 teaspoon dried savory
- 1/4 teaspoon dried basil
- pinch salt + pepper

Make it Vegan! *See Pro Tips*

Seasoning Blend
- 1/2 tablespoon ground sage
- 1 tablespoon poultry seasoning
- 1 teaspoon sea salt
- 1/2 teaspoon black pepper
- 1/2 teaspoon granulated onion
- 1 teaspoon celery salt
- 1/2 tablespoon chicken bouillon

- **1 8x8 pan cornbread, crumbled**
- **12 oz bread stuffing**
- **2 quarts chicken broth**
- **4 eggs, whisked**

Step-by-Step Instructions

- Measure & combine seasoning blend ingredients then set aside

- Whisk together eggs in a medium dish then set aside

- Add butter & cooking oil from sautée ingredients to a medium pot over medium/high heat until butter is melted

- Add remaining sautée ingredients to pot & cook until lightly golden brown, while stirring

- Add chicken broth to same sautée pot & bring to a light boil

- In a mixing bowl combine crumbled cornbread, classic stuffing & seasoning blend then mix to combine

- Very slowly pour in 3 cups of cooked broth into whisked eggs, while stirring continually

- Pour broth & egg mixture over seasoned cornbread & stuffing mix in mixing bowl & use rubber spatula to combine

- Gradually add remaining cooked broth to mixing bowl a few cups at a time while using a rubber spatula to combine

- Continue adding cooked broth to mixing bowl until dressing mixture is the consistency of thick grits

- Transfer dressing mixture to a baking dish & cover with foil

- Preheat oven to 350 degrees F

- Cook dressing covered for 40 minutes at 350 degrees F

- After 40 minutes remove from oven & allow cooked dressing to rest at least 15 minutes before serving

- Enjoy with gravy & cranberry sauce!

Pro Tips!

- Dressing will be loose but tighten up as it cooks

- You may not need to use all of the broth.

- Extra broth can be used in Homestyle Pan Gravy recipe.

- Slowly mixing the broth into the whisked eggs is called tempering; this will keep the hot broth from cooking the eggs if poured in all at once.

- Recipe can be doubled to make more servings.

Make It Vegan
- butter > coconut oil
- chicken broth > vegetable broth
- chicken bouillon > vegetable bouillon
- eggs > Just Egg®

CHEF'S HOMEMADE CRANBERRY SAUCE

There's a good chance you've never had Homemade Cranberry Sauce. Neither had I until just a few short years ago. We always used the canned, jellied stuff, which got the job done and done well. But trust me, once you've had fresh Homemade Cranberry Sauce, you will not want to go back to the can. It is perfectly sweet, slightly tart, and the texture is supreme. You really can eat it all by itself, it's that good. It's also much easier to make than you think & will have you wondering why you didn't make the switch sooner. Not to worry; the important thing is you're here now. So get ready to be made a believer and have your tastebuds blown away!

Ingredients

- 2 lbs frozen or fresh cranberries
- 3 cups white sugar
- 1/2 teaspoon sea salt
- 1-1/2 cups grape juice
- 1/2 tablespoon lemon juice

Step-by-Step Instructions

- Measure & add all ingredients to a medium sized pot

- Heat over medium/low heat while stirring to coat cranberries in sugar mixture

- Allow to come to a light boil & simmer for 20 minutes while stirring

- When cranberries begin to burst & syrup thickens, remove pot from heat

- Carefully transfer cooked cranberries & syrup to a high speed blender & blend until smooth

- Pour blended cranberry sauce through a mesh strainer over a mixing bowl, using a rubber spatula to push sauce through

- Discard the seeds & pulp from mesh strainer

- Transfer strained cranberry sauce to desired serving dish(es) and allow to cool completely in fridge to set (at least 4 hours)

- Serve with Cornbread Dressing & enjoy!

Pro Tips!

- Frozen cranberries work just as great as fresh.

- Fresh cranberries can be frozen in original packaging, with no additional prep work needed.

- Do not walk away from boiling/simmering cranberries; they will boil over & make a mess!

- Yes, you have to blend & strain cranberry sauce.

- Cranberry sauce will be hot so take care when blending; place a kitchen towel over blender cap hole so that steam can vent & top doesn't pop off.

- Adjust sweetness to taste by using more or less sugar.

- It's best to prepare cranberry sauce the day before to be fully set & chilled.

- Extra cranberry sauce can be frozen to use later.

CHEF'S HOMESTYLE PAN GRAVY

One time I made some Dressing but didn't make any gravy. I remember my grandmother politely asking where the gravy was? I told her I didn't have enough time, so I didn't make any. She indignantly replied, "Ain't no dressing ain't no gravy!" and she may or may not have pushed her plate away as she said it. I vowed at that moment to never again make Dressing without also making gravy, and neither should you. So even if you think you don't like gravy, here is the smoothest, richest, most savory gravy recipe you could ever find. Don't make the same mistake I did!

Ingredients

Seasoning Blend
- 1 teaspoon sea salt
- 1/2 teaspoon black pepper
- 1/2 tablespoon granulated onion
- 1 teaspoon granulated garlic
- 1/2 teaspoon celery salt
- 1/2 tablespoon chicken bouillon
- 1/4 cup flour

Wet Ingredients
- 4 cups beef broth
- drippings from cooked turkey

Sautée Ingredients
- 2 tablespoons butter
- 1/2 cup cooking oil
- 1 onion, sliced thin
- pinch of salt + pepper

Make It Vegan!
- butter > coconut oil
- chicken bouillon > vegetable bouillon
- beef broth > vegetable broth
- turkey drippings > liquid aminos

Step-by-Step Instructions

- Pre-measure seasoning blend ingredients into a single small dish & set aside

- In a large skillet or sauce pan cook sautée ingredients over medium/high heat for 7 minutes while stirring or until onions begin to lightly brown

- After 7 minutes add pre-measured seasoning ingredients & continue cooking 5 minutes while stirring until flour begins to lightly brown & foam

- Add wet ingredients while stirring or whisking until smooth

- Reduce heat to medium/low & simmer until gravy coats the back of a spoon or is thickened to your liking

- Adjust seasoning to taste & enjoy!

Pro Tips!

- Make your gravy gluten free by leaving out the flour & mixing 1/2 cup cornstarch with 1 cup of your broth of choice.

- Beef broth adds richer flavor & color but chicken or turkey broths work just fine if you prefer.

- Add a teaspoon of browning for color if you like your gravy darker.

- If gravy is too thick, add more broth to loosen.

- If gravy to too thin, continue to simmer over medium heat to tighten.

AUNTIE G'S DEVILED EGGS

Full disclosure: I have a of a love/hate relationship when it comes to eggs in general so I probably have only eaten Deviled Eggs a handful of times in my life. However in our family, everybody has their specialty dish that they make — which is usually one that they love to eat — and for my Auntie G, it's definitely Deviled Eggs. The family loves them and it seems like she can never make enough. Even though they aren't a must have for me, my recipe is stamped and approved to be a hit for your Thanksgiving table. Perfectly boiled eggs with a creamy, tangy filling, topped with sweet candied bacon? Sign me up!

Ingredients

- **12 medium eggs, hard boiled**
- **1 teaspoon baking soda**

Wet Ingredients
- 1/4 cup sour cream
- 1/4 cup mayonnaise
- 2 oz cream cheese, softened
- 1/2 tablespoon fresh lemon juice
- 1 tablespoon bread & butter pickle juice
- 1/2 tablespoon yellow mustard

Seasoning Blend
- 1/2 teaspoon sea salt
- 1/4 teaspoon black pepper
- 1/4 teaspoon granulated onion
- 1/4 teaspoon granulated garlic
- 2 teaspoons white sugar

Garnish
- paprika
- chopped fresh chives
- candied bacon squares

Step-by-Step Instructions

Boil the Eggs
- Carefully place eggs in a pot & cover with cold water + baking soda
- Bring pot to a rolling boil then cover & remove from heat
- Let eggs sit in covered pot of hot water for 12 min before transferring cooked eggs to a bowl with ice & water to cool

Peel the Eggs
- Carefully peel the shells off the cooled eggs (here is where the baking soda helps) & rinse peeled eggs under cold water to remove any broken bits of shell

Slice the Eggs
- Evenly slice the peeled eggs lengthwise to reveal the cooked yolk
- Carefully scoop out the cooked yolk from each half into a mixing bowl & set the cooked egg whites aside

Devil the Eggs
- Use a fork to mash cooked yolks in mixing bowl as finely as possible
- Measure & add all wet ingredients
- Measure & add seasoning blend ingredients
- Use an electric hand mixer to whip filling until smooth
- Use a small spoon or piping bag to fill each sliced egg white with the whipped mixture

Garnish the Eggs
- Sprinkle filled eggs with paprika & chopped fresh chives
- Brush 4 strips of uncooked bacon on both sides with a mix of brown sugar & maple syrup then cut into 1-2" squares
- Cook candied bacon squares on sheet pan in oven at 350 deg for 15 min or until crispy
- Allow bacon to cool then garnish each deviled egg with candied bacon square
- Serve deviled eggs well chilled & with a splash of hot sauce or crushed red pepper flakes for spice!

Pro Tips!

- Yes, use medium eggs instead of large or extra large.

- The baking soda helps the egg shells to easily peel off.

- Recipe can be doubled to make more servings.

- Substitute plain greek yogurt for sour cream to reduce fat.

COUSIN COCO'S POTATO SALAD

Who made the Potato Salad? One thing is for certain and two things for sure, you will not find any raisins in the Potato Salad at our holiday table because Cousin Coco holds it down! She is the type of cook that can taste a bite of something and accurately tell you every single ingredient in the recipe. It really is a gift. So when she tasted my Potato Salad and gave it her stamp of approval, I knew I had passed the vibe check. The secret? Cooking the potatoes just right so they're not too firm and not too mushy. Get into my winning recipe so if someone asks the question, you'll know it's no shade!

Ingredients

- **2.5 lbs yukon gold potatoes, cubed**
- **1 tablespoon sea salt**
- **2 large eggs, hardboiled, diced**

Wet Ingredients
- 1/2 cup mayonnaise
- 2 oz cream cheese
- 1 tablespoon dill pickle juice
- 1/4 cup sweet relish
- 2 tablespoons yellow mustard
- 1 tablespoon dijon mustard

Seasoning Blend
- 1/2 teaspoon paprika
- 1/2 teaspoon sea salt
- 1/2 teaspoon black pepper
- 1 teaspoon seasoned salt
- 1 teaspoon celery salt
- 1 teaspoon granulated onion
- 1/2 teaspoon granulated garlic
- 2 tablespoons white sugar

Mix-Ins
- 1/2 tablespoon fresh dill leaves
- 2 tablespoons diced pimentos
- 2 tablespoons diced celery
- 2 tablespoons diced onion

Step-by-Step Instructions

- Wash, peel & cut potatoes in 3/4" cubes before adding to empty pot with sea salt then covering potatoes by 1/2" with cold water

- Bring pot to a boil over medium heat & let cook for 8-10 minutes once boiling

- While potatoes are cooking combine all wet ingredients in a large mixing bowl & set aside

- Combine all seasoning blend ingredients in a small dish & set aside

- After boiling 8-10 minutes drain cooked potatoes & rinse under cold water

- Add seasoning blend to mixing bowl with wet ingredients & fold in

- Add mix-ins & diced hard boiled eggs to mixing bowl with seasoned wet ingredients & fold in

- Add cooked potatoes to mixing bowl with other ingredients & gently fold in until potatoes are well coated

- Adjust seasoning to taste before allowing potato salad to chill in fridge a minimum 4 hours or overnight

- Garnish chilled potato salad generously with paprika & enjoy!

Pro Tips!

- Be careful not to over cook potatoes & end up making mashed potato salad!

- Use your favorite potato variety in place of yukon gold if you prefer

- Yes, start boiling potatoes cold water, in order to cook more evenly

Make It Vegan!
- mayonnaise > plant based
- cream cheese > plant based
- hard boiled eggs > extra firm tofu

MOMMY'S BAKED MAC 'N CHEESE

If my grandmother was the queen of Cornbread Dressing, then my mother — yes, I still say Mommy — is the queen of Baked Mac 'n Cheese! So much so that I remember my grandmother once saying she won't even bother to make it since my mother's is so good. Now that I think about it, I don't remember my mother ever making Dressing either, so I guess they both agreed on those dishes.

While the great debate of roux vs. eggs in Mac 'n Cheese continues, I opt for the latter, even though Mommy's recipe doesn't. See, my Grandma Hattie made hers old school with eggs and I always loved her version too. So my recipe combines the best of both worlds to create a seasoned, creamy, cheesy, custardy Baked Mac 'n Cheese that will leave you & your loved ones scraping the pan!

Ingredients

5 Cheese Blend
- 8 oz block sharp cheddar cheese
- 16 oz block colby jack cheese
- 8 oz block provolone cheese
- 8 oz block medium cheddar cheese, for topping

Wet Ingredients
- 2 cups evaporated milk
- 1 cup heavy cream
- 4 eggs, beaten
- 2 tablespoons butter, melted
- 1 tablespoon yellow mustard

- **1 lb dried elbow macaroni noodles, boiled**

Seasoning Blend
- 2 teaspoons sea salt
- 2 teaspoons black pepper
- 1/4 teaspoon white pepper
- 1 tablespoon seasoned salt
- 2 teaspoons paprika

Garnish
- fresh chopped parsley

Make It Vegan! *See Pro Tips*

Step-by-Step Instructions

Boil Mac Noodles
- Bring 5 quarts water to a boil in a pot on medium heat
- Add 2 tablespoons sea salt to boiling water
- Add 1 cup evaporated milk to boiling water
- Add 1 lb elbow mac noodles & boil 20 min on medium heat while stirring occasionally
- Drain boiled mac noodles in strainer but do not rinse
- Shake off excess water & set cooked noodles aside in strainer to continue draining

Shred Cheeses
- Shred block of medium cheddar cheese & set aside separately (we'll use this on top later)
- Shred remaining 4 blocks of cheese & set aside (it's okay to mix these together)

Mix Custard
- In a large mixing bowl whisk together all wet ingredients
- Measure & combine seasoning blend ingredients in a small dish
- Add already combined seasoning blend to mixing bowl with wet ingredients & whisk

Mix Mac
- Add cooked mac noodles to seasoned custard & fold in with rubber spatula to mix well
- Add mixed shredded 4 cheese blend to seasoned noodles & fold in to mix well
- Transfer mixed mac from mixing bowl to a large, deep baking dish

Cook Mac
- Preheat oven to 350 degrees F
- Cover with foil & bake covered at 350 degrees F for 35 minutes
- Remove from oven, uncover & add even layer of shredded medium cheddar cheese on top
- Return to oven uncovered & set oven to broil for 3-5 minutes
- Remove from oven & allow to rest 15 minutes before serving
- Garnish with fresh chopped parsley & enjoy!

Pro Tips!

- Yes, use block cheese & shred it fresh.

- Block provolone cheese can be cut fresh in the deli section.

- Yes, eggs do go in this recipe.

- Use regular size elbow macaroni noodles.

- Yes, boil mac noodles for 20 minutes.

- Keep an eye on the stove; do not let your pot boil over.

- Do not let your magnificent mac 'n cheese burn while on broil; set a timer & do not walk away!

- Recipe can be doubled to make more servings.

Make It Vegan!
- elbow macaroni noodles > plant based
- shredded cheese > vegan cheese and/or nutritional yeast
- evaporated milk > cashew milk
- heavy cream > coconut milk
- eggs > Just Egg®
- butter > coconut oil

COUSIN KIM'S CANDIED YAMS

Candied yams, sweet potatoes or whatever you want to call them, Cousin Kim set the bar when it comes to this holiday staple! Not overly sweet, super syrupy & perfectly spiced, it seems like she can never make enough — because we absolutely need leftovers! I remember asking Cousin Kim for her recipe and of course she cooks with nothing but love and vibes so no ingredients were measured! She told me things like, a bag of sugar, a bottle of vanilla extract, and an assortment of aromatic spices like cinnamon, ginger & nutmeg. What size bag? How big of a bottle? A teaspoon or tablespoon? All questions that needed answers! But don't worry...I've done all the hard work and perfected my recipe for you to share at your holiday table.

Ingredients

- **4 lbs sweet potatoes, cut**
- **1/2 stick butter, cubed**

Seasoning Blend
- 2 cups white sugar
- 1 cup brown sugar
- 4 tablespoons cornstarch
- 1 teaspoon sea salt
- 1 teaspoon ground cinnamon
- 1/2 teaspoon ground nutmeg
- 1/4 teaspoon ground ginger

Wet Ingredients
- 2 tablespoons pineapple juice
- 1 tablespoon pure vanilla extract
- 1 tablespoon molasses
- 1 teaspoon lemon juice

Make It Vegan!
- butter > coconut oil

Step-by-Step Instructions

- Measure & combine seasoning blend in a dish and set aside

- Measure & combine wet ingredients in a dish & set aside

- Rinse, peel & cut sweet potatoes into desired shape (cubes, circles, half circles, etc.)

- Carefully add cut sweet potatoes to pot of boiling water

- Boil sweet potatoes for 8-10 minutes then drain & rinse under cold water until cool

- Add boiled & cooled sweet potatoes to a mixing bowl, along with seasoning blend & wet ingredients

- Using a rubber spatula, gently mix all ingredients until well combined

- Wet & dry ingredients will form a rich syrup once properly mixed

- Transfer mixed sweet potatoes to a baking dish & evenly add cubed butter pieces on top

- Preheat oven to 350 degrees F

- Cover baking dish with foil and cook sweet potatoes for 40 minutes at 350 degrees

- After 40 minutes remove baking dish from oven & use rubber spatula to gently mix & stir cooking sweet potatoes

- Cover & return to oven for additional 40 minutes or until sweet potatoes are fork tender.

- Transfer sweet potatoes to a baking dish & enjoy!

Pro Tips!

- Yes, boil sweet potatoes first.

- Be careful not to over cook sweet potatoes when boiling.

- Cut about 1/2" off ends of sweet potatoes before peeling, to make peeling easier

- Cut sweet potatoes in half crosswise first & cut into preferred shape from there, since sweet potato shapes & sizes can be irregular.

- Sweet potatoes can be cut into any preferred shape; just be sure to keep size of cuts as consistent as possible

- Allow sweet potatoes to cook as long as neccessary to become fork tender; taking them out too soon will result in less developed flavor & texture.

- Recipe can be doubled to make more servings.

CHEF'S GARLIC PARMESAN MASHED POTATOES

Mashed Potatoes...to be or not to be at the Thanksgiving table? That is the question. In our family the answer is yes! When you're serving up dishes like Uncle Steve's Smothered Beef Roast or my Homestyle Pan Gravy, those are reason enough to justify having Mashed Potatoes on the menu. And when they're as good as my Garlic Parmesan Mashed Potatoes, you won't want to wait for just the holidays to make them. We're ditching the boxed dried stuff to make the freshest, creamiest, tastiest Mashed Potatoes you've had so far!

Ingredients

- **2.5 lbs yukon gold potatoes, peeled**
- **1 tablespoon sea salt**
- **6 cloves garlic, peeled**
- **1/2 onion, diced**

Wet Ingredients
- 1 stick butter
- 1 cup heavy cream
- 1 cup sour cream
- 8 oz block parmesan cheese, shredded

Seasoning Blend
- 1 tablespoon sea salt
- 1/2 teaspoon black pepper
- 1 tablespoon chicken bouillon
- 1/2 tablespoon dried savory
- 2 teaspoons granulated garlic
- 1 teaspoon granulated onion

Make It Vegan!
- butter > coconut oil
- heavy cream > cashew milk
- sour cream > coconut milk
- parmesan cheese > vegan cheese and/or nutritional yeast
- chicken bouillon > vegetable

Step-by-Step Instructions

- Wash & peel potatoes before adding to empty pot with sea salt, garlic & onions then covering potatoes by 1/2" with cold water

- Bring pot to a boil over medium heat & let cook for 25 minutes once boiling

- While potatoes are cooking combine butter, heavy cream to a small pan & heat just until butter melts

- Combine all seasoning blend ingredients in a small dish & set aside

- After boiling 25 minutes drain cooked potatoes, onion, garlic in strainer then transfer all to large mixing bowl

- Pour melted butter mixture over potatoes in mixing bowl & use potato masher to mash

- Add sour cream & already combined seasoning blend to mixing bowl & continue to mash

- Add freshly shredded parmesan cheese to mixing bowl & use rubber spatula to fold in until well combined

- Use whisk or electric hand mixer to whip potatoes until smooth

- Transfer whipped potatoes to a serving dish, garnish & enjoy!

Pro Tips!

- Use your favorite potato variety in place of yukon gold if you prefer.

- Peel as little or as much skin as you prefer in your mashed potatoes.

- Yes, start boiling potatoes cold water in order to cook more evenly.

- Yes, use fresh shredded parmesan cheese.

- Yes, heat up your butter & heavy cream first to keep potatoes hot while whipping up.

- For chunkier mashed potatoes, skip the whisk/hand mixer.

CHEF'S GARLIC BUTTER GREEN BEANS

Now some may say, who needs Green Beans when you've got Collard Greens on the table? Green Beans tend to get a bad wrap when it comes to the holiday menu — looking at you Green Bean Casserole! Some Thanksgiving dishes just require the bright, savory flavor of garden fresh Garlic Butter Green Beans to go along with them. This recipe is sure to make even the biggest skeptic a believer. Thank me later, once you've got that tender a juicy slice of Oven Roasted Turkey, some creamy Parmesan Garlic Mashed Potatoes & Homestyle Gravy on your plate!

Ingredients

- **3 lbs fresh or frozen whole green beans**

Stock Ingredients
- 6 cloves garlic, chopped
- 1/2 red onion, sliced thin
- 2 turkey tails
- 1/2 stick butter, cubed
- 4 cups chicken broth

Garnish
- sliced grape tomatoes
- pad of butter

Seasoning Blend
- 1 teaspoon sea salt
- 1 teaspoon black pepper
- 1/2 tablespoon seasoned salt
- 2 tablespoons granulated onion
- 1 tablespoon granulated garlic
- 1/2 teaspoon paprika
- 1/4 teaspoon nutmeg
- 1/2 tablespoon chicken bouillon

Make It Vegan!
- butter > coconut oil
- chicken bouillon > vegetable
- turkey tails > liquid smoke
- chicken broth > vegetable

Step-by-Step Instructions

- If using fresh green beans, prep by trimming ends and rinsing

- Measure & combine seasoning blend ingredients in a separate dish and set aside

- Add stock ingredients to a large pot & bring to a boil over medium heat

- Once boiling, add green beans to pot & use tongs to toss & coat green beans in stock liquid

- Cover pot & boil over medium heat for 20-30 minutes or until green beans reach desired tenderness

- After cooking 20-30 minutes adjust seasoning to taste

- Transfer green beans to a serving dish, garnish & enjoy!

Pro Tips!

- Frozen green beans work just as great as fresh.

- Green beans are starchy, so they require a good amount of seasoning for the flavor to stick; adjust seasonings to your taste.

- Tukey tails can be left whole or broken down with the meat mixed into the green beans if you prefer.

- For a hint of spice, add your favorite cajun seasoning or cayenne pepper to taste.

TT DAWN'S COLLARD GREENS

If my grandmother was the greens queen, then my sister, TT Dawn — as my two young sons affectionately call her — is the heir apparent! Collard Greens is one of those recipes that is a true labor of love to properly prepare. From selecting or fresh picking your greens, to cleaning them — and cleaning them again — to seasoning and then slow cooking them just right, it truly is an art. It takes so much work and time that if they don't turn out right it can be gut wrenching. TT Dawn has gotten it right time & time again! Her Collard Greens are full of only the freshest leafy greens, no stems, perfectly seasoned, and slick! Now if you don't know what slick greens are, you're about to find out. Even though TT Dawn won't share her actual recipe with me, I've put together my own version that just might put me on the throne next!

Ingredients

- **4 bunches fresh collard greens, stems removed, cut & washed well**
- **1/2 cup white vinegar**
- **1/2 tablespoon baking soda**

Stock Ingredients
- 1/2 onion
- 2 turkey tails
- 1/2 stick butter
- 1 tablespoon worcestershire sauce

Seasoning Blend
- 1/2 tablespoon sea salt
- 1 teaspoon black pepper
- 1/2 tablespoon seasoned salt
- 1 teaspoon cajun seasoning
- 2 tablespoons granulated onion
- 1 tablespoon granulated garlic
- 1 teaspoon paprika
- 1 tablespoon chicken bouillon
- 1/2 cup brown sugar

Make It Vegan! *See Pro Tips*

Step-by-Step Instructions

- Prep bunches of collard green leaves by removing center stem, stacking leaves, rolling then cutting greens into 2" strips

- Wash prepped greens in clean sink filled with luke warm water & 2 tablespoons of baking soda, rinse well with cold water & repeat

- Measure & combine seasoning blend ingredients in a small dish and set aside

- Add stock ingredients & already measured seasoning blend to a large pot & bring to a boil over medium heat

- Once boiling, add greens to pot & use tongs to coat greens in stock liquid

- Cover & boil over medium/low heat for 60-75 minutes or until greens reach desired tenderness

- After cooking 60-75 minutes adjust seasoning to taste

- Sprinkle baking soda over cooked greens in pot

- Evenly pour white vinegar over cooked greens in pot

- Vinegar & baking soda will bubble up & greens can be tossed with tongs to mix in

- Transfer greens to a serving dish & enjoy!

Pro Tips!

- Yes, use fresh brunches of collard greens.

- No, do not use bagged & cut greens.

- No, do not use frozen greens.

- No, do not use canned greens.

- Yes, remove stems from the greens (unless you enjoy them, of course).

- Greens are starchy, so they require a good amount of seasoning for the flavor to stick; adjust seasonings to your taste.

- Tukey tails can be left whole or broken down with the meat mixed into the greens if you prefer.

- Baking soda & vinegar work to "remove the gas" from the collard greens as well as help tenderize and make less acidic.

CHEF'S BUTTERMILK CORNBREAD

Is it sweet? Most people I know feel a strong way about the type of cornbread that they like. Sweet cornbread definitely has it place, but for my family's holiday table, classic buttermilk cornbread is it! This is a bonus recipe because you can use it to make your Cornbread Dressing or eat it with those good Collard Greens or if you are really with the vibes, crumbled up in a bowl with buttermilk poured over top plus a pinch of sugar. IYKYK!

Ingredients

Dry Mix
- 1 cup yellow cornmeal
- 3/4 cup ap flour
- 1/4 cup white sugar
- 1 tablespoon cornstarch
- 1 teaspoon sea salt
- 1/2 teaspoon baking soda
- 1/2 teaspoon baking powder

Wet Ingredients
- 1/2 cup buttermilk
- 2 eggs
- 2 tablespoons melted butter
- 1/4 cup hot water

Make It Vegan!
- buttermilk > coconut milk
- eggs > Just Egg®
- butter > coconut oil

Step-by-Step Instructions

- Measure & combine dry mix ingredients in a mixing bowl

- Add wet ingredients one at a time in order, mixing lightly with a whisk to combine after each ingredient is added

- Preheat oven to 350 degrees F

- Place 8" cast iron pan or 8x8 baking dish in oven for 10 min with 2 tablespoons cooking oil in pan

- Remove cast iron pan or baking dish from oven and pour in mixed cornbread

- Carefully tap cast iron pan or baking dish on counter 5 times to remove air bubbles

- Bake cornbread for 25 minutes at 350 degrees F or until golden brown around edges & separating from sides of pan

- Top with butter, slice & enjoy or use for Cornbread Dressing!

Pro Tips!

- This recipe is best for making Cornbread Dressing, enjoying with Collard Greens, or on its own.

- No, this isn't a sweet or Jiffy style cornbread.

- For a sweet, Jiffy style cornbread, increase sugar to 1 cup, flour to 1 cup & reduce eggs to just 1.

- Yes, heat oil in cast iron pan or baking dish first; creates a wonderfully crispy edge.

I thought you said you can't bake?

Now I never said I *can't* bake...just that I *don't.* Not usually. But for you and this cookbook, I am making an exception!

A chef who can confidently whip up both savory and sweet dishes is a rare breed. Why do you think strictly Pastry Chefs exist? Normally you'll find chefs that have mastered one or the other, but rarely both.

It's me. I'm chefs! While I don't *usually* bake, there are a few baking recipes I have made it a point to master. Those recipes are largely the ones that satisfy my own sweet tooth, and today, I am so excited to share those with you!

The baking recipes that follow have been proven tried and true in my own kitchen with my loved ones...and they are a tough audience! That means all of the experimenting and guesswork have been done for you. Because baking can be a bit of a drama — it's either a total hit or a complete disaster. There is no in between!

And who wants to deal with all that after spending so much time, effort, and ingredients in the kitchen? Unlike savory dishes where you can add a pinch of this or a dash of that to rescue a recipe, there is no saving a failed baked good. Baking really is an exact science!

So thanks again for choosing to let my holiday cookbook guide your #foodlove and enjoy these sweet recipes that I am so happy to share with you as a part of my #VibeTribe!

@chefmikehard

NANNY'S SWEET POTATO PIE

Fun fact: I have never eaten pumpkin pie before! Not that I have anything against it, but for my family's holiday table, Sweet Potato Pie reigns supreme. I also have nothing against Auntie Patti, but Nanny's Sweet Potato Pie was known near and far as one of the best slices you could ever taste! The texture was smooth, creamy, not overly sweet and had the perfect filling to crust ratio which is super important for a good Sweet Potato Pie. Now I never learned Nanny's exact recipe, but over the years I have perfected my own version that checks all the boxes and I have been told that it is a solid stand-in for Nanny's. So after you've had a plate or three for dinner, make sure to save room for a piece of Nanny's Sweet Potato Pie. And don't forget the whipped cream on top!

Ingredients

- **1 prepared 9" pie crust**
- **2 cups mashed sweet potatoes (about 3 medium potatoes)**
- **1 cup white sugar**

Spice Blend
- 1/2 teaspoon ground cinnamon
- 1/4 teaspoon ground nutmeg
- 1/4 teaspoon ground allspice
- 1/8 teaspoon ground ginger
- 1/4 teaspoon sea salt

Wet Ingredients
- 1 stick butter, softened
- 2 large eggs
- 1/2 cup evaporated milk
- 1 tablespoon molasses
- 1 teaspoon pure vanilla extract
- 1/2 teaspoon lemon juice

Make It Vegan!
- butter > coconut oil
- eggs > Just Egg®
- milk > coconut milk

Step-by-Step Instructions

- Preheat your oven to 350 degrees F

- Bake washed sweet potatoes in preheated oven on a sheet tray for about 45-60 minutes or until they are soft and easily pierced with a fork

- Remove from the oven and allow sweet potatoes to cool

- In a large mixing bowl, scoop out the flesh of the sweet potatoes and mash them until smooth

- In a separate mixing bowl whisk to combine Wet ingredients until even consistency is reached

- To the mashed sweet potatoes add combined Wet ingredients followed by already measured Spice Blend

- Mix everything together until the filling is well combined and smooth.

- Pour the sweet potato filling into prepared pie crust, spreading it out evenly.

- Place the pie in the preheated oven and bake for 50-60 minutes, or until the filling is set

- After 50-60 minutes allow pie to cool on a wire rack for at least an hour

- Once it has cooled to room temperature, you can transfer it to the refrigerator for a few hours or overnight to chill and set completely

- Serve your sweet potato pie as is or enjoy with a dollop of whipped cream or a scoop of vanilla ice cream for an extra treat!

Pro Tips!

- Select sweet potatoes that are fresh, firm, and have vibrant orange flesh. These will be sweeter and result in a more flavorful pie. Avoid using canned sweet potatoes for the best flavor.

- To ensure even baking, make sure your sweet potatoes are uniformly cooked. Place them on a sheet tray rather than directly on the oven grates to catch any drips.

- To achieve a silky smooth texture for your filling, use a food processor or immersion blender to puree the sweet potatoes. This will remove any lumps and create a creamy consistency.

- Adjust the spices to your taste. Some people prefer a bit more cinnamon or nutmeg, so feel free to adjust these seasonings to match your preference.

- Allow the butter and eggs to come to room temperature before mixing them into the filling. This ensures they incorporate more evenly with the sweet potatoes.

- Keep a close eye on your pie towards the end of the baking time. Over baking can cause cracks in the pie. It's ready when the center is set but still slightly jiggly.

- Wrap the edge of yout pie crust with foil to keep from browning too quickly while baking.

- For the best texture and flavor, let your sweet potato pie chill in the refrigerator for a few hours or overnight. This allows the flavors to meld and the filling to set properly, making it easier to slice and serve.

7 UP®
POUND
CAKE

When it came to the kitchen, Nanny could do all things! Including baking and especially Pound Cake. I think that's due in part to my grandfather — who we called Pa Pa — having a strong sweet tooth. He loved his sweets after a nice savory meal and Nanny obliged. One of his and everyone else's favorites was Nanny's Pound Cake. And she did it the classic, old school way: one pound of this, one pound of that, a little razzle dazzle and boom! It was always moist with a nice full crumb and that undeniable homemade Pound Cake flavor. Forget the fork for this one...it tastes better when you break off pieces and eat it with your fingers. I don't make the rules, but I do make a mean 7 UP® Pound Cake, just like Nanny did!

Ingredients

- 2 sticks butter, softened
- 3 cups white sugar
- 5 large eggs
- 3 cups ap flour
- 1/2 cup 7 UP® soda
- 1/4 cup heavy cream

- 1/2 tablespoon vanilla extract
- 1/2 teaspoon lemon extract
- 1/4 teaspoon almond extract
- powdered sugar for dusting

Make It Vegan!
- heavy cream > coconut milk
- eggs > Just Egg®
- butter > coconut oil

Step-by-Step Instructions

- Preheat your oven to 325 degrees F

- Grease and flour a 10" bundt pan

- In a large mixing bowl, cream the softened butter, heavy cream, and sugar together until light and fluffy, about 5-7 minutes

- Add the eggs one at a time, mixing well after each addition, making sure to scrape down the sides of the bowl to ensure even mixing

- Gradually add the flour and 7 UP® soda to the butter and egg mixture, starting and ending with the flour

- Mix until just combined, being careful not to over mix

- Gently stir in the vanilla, lemon, and almond extracts until just combined

- Pour batter into the prepared bundt pan, smoothing the top with a lightly greased rubber spatula

- Bake in preheated oven for 60-70 minutes, or until a toothpick inserted into the center comes out clean

- Allow the cake to cool in the pan for 15-20 minutes, then invert it onto a wire rack, removing pan, to cool completely

- Once the cake has cooled, use a mesh strainer to dust with powdered sugar, slice, serve, and enjoy!

Pro Tips!

- Use room temperature ingredients for the best results.

- Be patient when creaming the butter and sugar; it's key to a light and fluffy cake.

- Alternate adding the dry ingredients and 7 UP®, starting and ending with the dry ingredients.

- Don't over mix the batter once the flour is added; just mix until combined.

- Be careful with the extracts they add wonderful flavor but can be overpowering if you use too much.

- Ensure the bundt pan is well greased and floured to prevent sticking.

- Allow the cake to cool before slicing for the best texture and flavor.

- An over baked cake is a dry cake. Check for doneness after 50-55 minutes or when cake scent becomes highly fragrant from the oven.

WHIPPED BANANA PUDDING

Is it really Banana Pudding if there's no bananas in it? One Thanksgiving my father showed me his mother's Banana Pudding recipe. Made from scratch, old school style with the custard, meringue & everything. Now that's a special occasion recipe because it takes some serious time and effort. But my Whipped Banana Pudding recipe you can make quick, easy and it's so good.

One thing I think we can all agree on is that ain't nothing wrong with extra *extra* cookies, so my recipe is loaded with all the cookies for whichever way you like it. And whether you like actual bananas in yours or not, my Whipped Banana Pudding recipe is worth giving a try. Because the truth is, it won't last long enough on your holiday table for those bananas to have a chance to even turn brown!

Ingredients

- 1 box Nilla® wafers
- 1 pack Golden Oreos®
- 1 pack Chessmen® Cookies
- 1 pack vanilla wafers
- 1 ripe banana

whipped cream
- 1 quart heavy cream
- 1-1/2 cups powdered sugar
- 1 tablespoon vanilla extract

Pudding Ingredients
- 3 boxes Jell-O® banana cream pudding (3.4 oz each)
- 1 quart half 'n half
- 2 tablespoons vanilla extract
- 1/2 cup sweetened condensed milk

Make It Vegan!
- whipped cream > plant based
- half 'n half > coconut milk
- condensed milk > coconut cream

Step-by-Step Instructions

- Add all Pudding ingredients to mixing bowl & whisk (or use hand mixer) until well combined then set aside

- In a separate mixing bowl (or stand mixer) add all Whipped Cream ingredients and whip on low speed, gradually increasing to med/high speed until stiff peaks form (about 6-8 minutes).

- Add whipped cream to prepared pudding and gently fold in then whisk until well combined *Optional: fold in confetti sprinkles for a fun color pop!*

- Peel & slice 1 banana into 1/8" pieces (we like it heavy on the cookies and light on the bananas over here!)

- Layer whipped pudding, Nilla® wafers and bananas in your serving dish and repeat one more time

- Top with remaining whipped pudding, spreading out evenly, then crumbled Nilla® wafers, optional caramel sauce, whole Nilla® wafers, Golden Oreos®, Chessmen® Cookies and vanilla wafers

- Allow to chill in refrigerator at least 4 hours or overnight before serving to soften cookies & enjoy!

Pro Tips!

- Use ripe bananas for the best flavor. They should have brown speckles on the skin, which indicates sweetness and a stronger banana flavor.

- Toss the banana slices in a bit of lemon juice to prevent them from browning.

- For the fluffiest texture, make your whipped cream from heavy cream. Whipped cream from a can or frozen whipped topping won't provide the same light and airy consistency.

- To ensure the whipped cream is at its best, place the mixing bowl and beaters in the refrigerator or freezer for about 15 minutes before whipping the cream. Cold equipment helps the cream whip faster and hold its shape.

- When folding the whipped cream into the pudding mixture, use a gentle hand and fold until just combined. Overmixing can deflate the whipped cream and result in a denser pudding.

- To create a visually appealing dessert, consider layering the banana pudding in individual serving cups or glasses. This allows you to showcase the delicious layers of pudding, bananas, and whipped cream.

- For the best flavor and texture, refrigerate the banana pudding for a few hours or overnight before serving. This allows the flavors to meld and the dessert to set properly.

BROWN BUTTER PEACH COBBLER

So the truth is, I haven't always loved peach cobbler. If you're like me, there's just something about warm, mushy fruit that doesn't quite sit right on the palate. But hear me out! Both my Nanny and Grandma Hattie used to make an amazing peach cobbler. There was just something about that crust, warm spiced peachy syrup, and don't let there be some vanilla ice cream involved! Needless to say, peach cobbler has evolved into one of my favorite desserts to enjoy, large in part due to my brother from another mother, Mama Phyllis' flawless version. My Brown Butter Peach Cobbler takes things up a notch with the deep flavor of brown butter and a splash of peach whiskey for perfectly cooked, super flavorful peaches. And since we love the syrup and crust over here, there's plenty of that goodness to enjoy with my recipe. Just remember, vanilla ice cream is a must!

Ingredients

- **4 cups frozen peach slices (or fresh if preferred)**
- **4 tablespoons butter (1/2 stick)**
- **2 sheets of ready-made pie crust**
- **1/4 cup butter, melted**
- **2 tablespoons cinnamon + white sugar (for sprinkling)**

Spice Blend
- 1 cup white sugar
- 1/4 cup brown sugar

1/2 teaspoon ground cinnamon
1/4 teaspoon ground nutmeg
1/4 teaspoon sea salt
1 tablespoon cornstarch

Wet Ingredients
- 1 teaspoon vanilla extract
- 1 teaspoon lemon juice
- 2 tablespoons peach whiskey

Make It Vegan!
- butter > coconut oil
- pie crust > plant based

Step-by-Step Instructions

- Preheat your oven to 350 degrees F

- In a large saucepan, melt butter over medium heat while stirring until lightly browned and fragrant, about 5-7 minutes

- Add peaches along with Wet ingredients and Spice Blend

- Cook over medium heat, stirring frequently, until the mixture thickens and the peaches are tender, about 8-10 minutes

- Remove from heat and set aside

- Line the bottom of a 9x13-inch baking dish with one sheet of ready-made pie crust, allowing it to overlap the sides of the dish

- Pour the cooked peach mixture into the crust-lined baking dish

- Place the second sheet of pie crust over the peaches

- You can create a lattice or simply crimp the edges to seal the cobbler (no lattice means more crust!)

- Brush the melted butter over the top pie crust then sprinkle cinnamon + sugar mixture

- Bake in preheated oven for 30-40 minutes, or until the crust is golden brown and the peach filling is bubbling

- Allow the cobbler to cool slightly before serving

- Serve with a scoop of vanilla bean ice cream and enjoy!

Pro Tips!

- If using fresh peaches, make sure they are ripe and sweet for the best flavor.

- Adjust the amount of sugar to suit your taste, depending on the sweetness of the peaches.

- Consider thawing and draining frozen peaches to prevent excess liquid in the filling.

- Don't overfill the pie crust, as the filling will expand while baking.

- You can create a decorative lattice pattern with the second pie crust for an extra touch of Southern charm.

- Brushing the crust with melted butter enhances its flavor and texture and helps the crust brown evenly.

STRAWBERRY CRUNCH CHEESECAKE

Cheesecake. Most people either love it or hate it. For me it's always been all love. I grew up seeing Nanny make Cheesecakes by the dozen it seems, because everybody knew hers were the best! Nanny's Cheesecake was one of the only dessert recipes I ever learned directly from her. She always did things the same way, every time — something else in the kitchen I learned from her — so Nanny's Cheesecake came out consistently good every single time. Even though, she would always offer the disclaimer "now...this might not be my best," it seemed like they got better than her best each time and were always good. So when you make my Strawberry Crunch Cheesecake recipe, don't worry; it will absolutely be your best. Enjoy!

Ingredients

- 3 blocks cream cheese, softened
- 2 ready-made graham cracker crusts
- 1-1/2 cups white sugar
- 1/2 teaspoon sea salt
- 3 large eggs
- 2 teaspoons vanilla extract

Strawberry Crunch
- 1 pack Golden Oreo Thins®
- 1/2 cup freeze dried strawberry powder

- 1/4 cup ap flour
- 1/4 cup heavy cream
- 1 cup sour cream
- 2 tablespoons pineapple juice

Make It Vegan!
- cream cheese > plant based
- eggs > Just Egg®
- heavy cream > coconut milk
- sour cream > plant based

Step-by-Step Instructions

- Add Strawberry Crunch ingredients to a bowl and crush with a potato masher to desired texture/crumb size, then set aside

- Preheat oven to 325 degrees F

- In a large mixing bowl, beat the softened cream cheese until it's smooth and creamy

- Gradually add sugar and continue to beat until the mixture is well combined

- Add eggs, one at a time, beating well after each addition

- Stir in vanilla extract, heavy cream, and pineapple juice

- Gently fold in the flour until the batter is smooth and creamy

- Gently fold in the sour cream until fully incorporated into the filling

- Pour the cheesecake filling into the ready-made graham cracker crust, spreading it out evenly

- Use a sheet tray or larger baking dish to create a water bath for cheesecake to bake in

- Place the water bath held cheesecake in preheated oven and bake for 50-60 minutes, or until the edges are set but the center is slightly jiggly

- After 50-60 minutes turn oven off and crack oven door, allowing cheesecake to naturally cool for 30-60 minutes

- After 30-60 minutes carefully remove water bath held cheesecake from oven

- Add even coating of Strawberry Crunch topping to cheesecake

- Allow the cheesecake to cool at room temperature for 1 hour on a wire rack, then refrigerate for at least 4 hours, or overnight, to set completely

- Slice, serve with whipped cream on top & enjoy!

Pro Tips!

- Use softened cream cheese for a smooth and creamy filling.

- Add the eggs one at a time and fold in ingredients gently to avoid over mixing, which can lead to cracking.

- Allow the cheesecake to cool slowly to prevent cracking. A gradual temperature change is key.

- A water bath can help prevent cracks simply place a roasting pan filled with hot water on the rack below the cheesecake in the oven.

- Be patient and let the cheesecake chill for the recommended time in the refrigerator to set properly.

BETTER THAN SCRATCH BOX BROWNIES

What if I told you these moist, chewy Chocolate Fudge Brownies were from the box & not made from scratch? To be honest, baking generally is not my thing. It takes so many ingredients, too much time and usually makes a mess with tons of dishes to wash. Then, you have to hope and pray it actually turns out good. So forget all that! I'll show you how to doctor up those box brownies with just a few simple ingredient hacks. You won't be able to tell that they weren't made from scratch and neither will anyone else. Save time in the kitchen this holiday season (or any time) with my stress free, can't miss Better Than Scratch Box Brownies recipe!

Ingredients

- 1 box brownie mix
- 1/2 cup walnuts, toasted & chopped
- 8 oz semi-sweet baking bar, chopped
- 1/8 teaspoon sea salt

Wet Ingredients
- 1/4 cup vegetable oil
- 1 egg

- 1 tablespoon heavy cream
- 2 tablespoons buttermilk
- 1/2 teaspoon instant coffee + 1 tablespoon hot water
- 1 teaspoon vanilla extract

Make It Vegan!
- buttermilk > coconut milk
- eggs > Just Egg®

Step-by-Step Instructions

- Start by preheating oven to 350 degrees F

- Coat an 8x8" baking dish with non-stick spray & line with parchment paper

- Next, toast your measured walnuts in a dry pan over medium heat until fragrant & beginning to brown

- Add measured dry ingredients to a mixing bowl

- Stir with rubber spatula to combine

- Add measured wet ingredients to mixing bowl

- Stir by hand with rubber spatula until well combined

- To avoid over mixing, do not use an electric stand or hand mixer

- Batter will be be thick & even in color when ready, with no dry spots

- Transfer mixed brownie batter to prepared baking dish

- Spread batter evenly in baking dish

- Bake according to box instructions for dish size & type

- Allow baked brownies to cool on baking rack for 30 minutes, plus an additional 30 minutes in refrigerator before cutting into squares

- Enjoy with vanilla bean ice cream, caramel sauce, chopped nuts, whipped cream & a cherry on top!

Pro Tips!

- Start with a high-quality brownie mix. Look for one that specifies "fudgy" or "chewy" on the packaging, as this will typically yield the best results.

- When combining the wet and dry ingredients, mix just until they are incorporated. Overmixing can lead to tough brownies.

- To easily remove the brownies from the pan and prevent sticking, line the baking pan with parchment paper, leaving an overhang on two sides. This also makes cleanup a breeze.

- To achieve a moist and chewy texture, consider underbaking the brownies by a minute or two. They will continue to set as they cool, and a slightly underbaked center will stay soft and fudgy.

- If you want ultra chewy brownies, place them in the refrigerator for an hour before slicing. This firms them up and makes them easier to cut cleanly.

- Store your brownies in an airtight container at room temperature. Placing a slice of bread in the container can help keep them moist, as the bread will absorb excess moisture and prevent the brownies from drying out.

DOUBLETREE® CHOCOLATE CHIP COOKIES

Have you ever been to the DoubleTree® Hotel and had one of their famous Chocolate Chip Cookies...even though you weren't staying there as a guest? Oh. Me either. Now as much as I claim that baking isn't my thing, I never said I couldn't bake, just that I don't...usually. But these DoubleTree® Chocolate Chip Cookies are worth the stress of it all and turn out so perfect every time. After all, what holiday season menu is complete without a warm, gooey, Chocolate Chip Cookie with a crispy edge and soft middle? Trust me, you'll be looking for any excuse to make these (better than) DoubleTree® Chocolate Chip Cookies during the holidays or any other time. Now pass the milk!

Ingredients

Wet Ingredients
- 2 sticks butter, browned
- 1-1/2 cups brown sugar
- 1/2 cup white sugar
- 1 egg, whole + 2 yolks
- 1 tablespoon vanilla extract
- 3 tablespoons heavy cream
- 1/4 teaspoon lemon juice
-
- **1 cup semi-sweet chocolate chips**
- **8 oz baking bar, chopped**
- **1-1/2 cups chopped walnuts**

Dry Ingredients
- 2 cups ap flour
- 1 tablespoon cornstarch
- 1/2 cup rolled oats
- 1 teaspoon sea salt
- 1 teaspooon baking soda
- 1/8 teaspoon cinnamon

Make It Vegan!
- butter > coconut oil
- eggs > Just Egg®
- heavy cream > cashew milk
- chocolate > dark or plant based

Step-by-Step Instructions

- Preheat oven to 325 degrees F

- In a mixing bowl, whisk together Dry ingredients then set dry mixture aside

- In a separate mixing bowl combine Wet ingredients and whisk together until smooth and creamy, about 3-4 minutes

- Gradually add the Dry ingredients to the Wet mixture, stirring until just combined, being careful not to over mix

- Gently fold in the semi-sweet chocolate chips and chopped walnuts until they are evenly distributed throughout the dough

- Drop rounded tablespoons of cookie dough onto baking sheet lined with parchment paper, leaving enough space between each for spreading

- Bake in the preheated oven for about 14-16 minutes, or until the edges are golden brown and the centers are still soft

- Allow the cookies to cool on the baking sheet for a few minutes before transferring them to a wire rack

- Serve cookies warm with a cold glass of milk & enjoy!

Pro Tips!

- Use room temperature wet ingredients for even mixing and proper texture.

- Whisking the dry ingredients helps ensure even distribution and a smoother dough.

- To keep the cookies soft and chewy, avoid over mixing the dough. Mix just until the ingredients are combined.

- For even better flavor, cover the cookie dough and refrigerate up to 24 hours before baking. This allows the flavors to meld. Remove from fridge about 30 minutes before baking.

- Use a small ice cream disher or similar for consistent sized and evenly baked cookies.

ABOUT THE AUTHOR

Meet Chef Mike Harden, the vibrant soul behind 'And Just Like That... Soulful Holiday Recipes Made Easy.' With a dash of passion and a sprinkle of inspiration drawn from the timeless traditions and secret recipes of his beloved grandmothers, Chef Mike Harden, known as @chefmikehard across social media, has brought his extraordinary culinary journey to life in his debut cookbook.

More than a decade of professional culinary experience has seasoned Chef Mike's expertise, but it is his entrepreneurial spirit that truly sets him apart. From bootstrapping his own food truck to orchestrating extravagant events with his full-service catering company and ultimately establishing the warm embrace of his very own restaurant, Chef Mike Harden's journey has been nothing short of an epic adventure.

What makes Chef Mike's recipes truly special is the way he weaves the warmth of tradition into every dish. 'And Just Like That... Soulful Holiday Recipes Made Easy' is a testament to his roots, a heart-warming tribute to his family, and a promise to readers that they too can master the art of soulful cooking in their own kitchens.

This cookbook isn't just a collection of recipes; it's an invitation to join Chef Mike on a culinary journey, guided by his expertise and his passion for making soulful cooking accessible to all. As you flip through these pages, you'll discover that cooking can be a celebration, a journey of love and flavor, and Chef Mike Harden is your trusted compass.

'And Just Like That... Soulful Holiday Recipes Made Easy' promises not only to make your holidays memorable but to inspire you to create your own culinary traditions, one unforgettable recipe at a time.

Made in the USA
Columbia, SC
19 November 2024

46966267R00058